HAL•LEONARD
INSTRUMENTAL
PLAY-ALONG

AUDIO
ACCESS
INCLUDED

PLAYBACK+
Speed • Pitch • Balance • Loop

THE GREATEST SHOWMAN

T0061488

Come Alive..2

From Now On..3

The Greatest Show 4

A Million Dreams 5

Never Enough...6

The Other Side 8

Rewrite the Stars 9

This Is Me 10

Tightrope..12

Audio Arrangements by Peter Deneff

To access audio visit:
www.halleonard.com/mylibrary

Enter Code
5696-7763-1030-9150

ISBN 978-1-5400-2841-9

HAL•LEONARD®
7777 W. BLUEMOUND RD. P.O.BOX 13819 MILWAUKEE, WI 53213

In Australia Contact:
Hal Leonard Australia Pty. Ltd.
4 Lentara Court
Cheltenham, Victoria, 3192 Australia
Email: ausadmin@halleonard.com.au

Visit Hal Leonard Online at
www.halleonard.com

COME ALIVE

CLARINET

Words and Music by BENJ PASEK
and JUSTIN PAUL

FROM NOW ON

Clarinet

Words and Music by BENJ PASEK
and JUSTIN PAUL

THE GREATEST SHOW

Clarinet

Words and Music by BENJ PASEK,
JUSTIN PAUL and RYAN LEWIS

A MILLION DREAMS

Clarinet

Words and Music by BENJ PASEK
and JUSTIN PAUL

NEVER ENOUGH

Clarinet

Words and Music by BENJ PASEK
and JUSTIN PAUL

THE OTHER SIDE

CLARINET

Words and Music by BENJ PASEK
and JUSTIN PAUL

REWRITE THE STARS

Clarinet

Words and Music by BENJ PASEK
and JUSTIN PAUL

THIS IS ME

CLARINET

Words and Music by BENJ PASEK
and JUSTIN PAUL

TIGHTROPE

CLARINET

Words and Music by BENJ PASEK
and JUSTIN PAUL